FROM THE
HEART

*Achieving Epic Results Through
Building a Heart-Based Culture of
Compassion and Empathy*

WADE THOMAS

ISBN: 978-1-7360465-0-0

This book is dedicated to the Leaders and Educators who dare to care.....for you are the ones who will change the world.

Contents

Introduction

Compassion and Empathy, isn't that for charitable organizations or new age well-doer's? It certainly is not for businesses who must fight the day to day battles in a competitive landscape that gets fiercer every year. Or is it? *From the Heart* will show you how a culture of compassion and empathy is not only a societal imperative, but how it will also provide your organization with a sustainable competitive advantage, no matter what industry you are in.

While I haven't always had the words for it, I have spent an entire career striving to bring compassion and empathy into cultures, lives, and my own leadership approach. Perhaps this was a result of my own belief system, but more importantly, I took this approach for one very practical reason. It works. I experienced great results, and the steep career trajectory that comes with it, for one simple reason. It works. I am confident that leading from the heart, and building a culture to match, will work for you as well.

The mission of this book is to help set your organization on the path to a heart-based culture. A culture that will lead to better relationships with your employees, vendors, and customers. A culture that will lead to sustainable business success and growth. Is your business ready for the challenge? Are you ready to step up to the opportunities that this culture will open up for you?

I wish you my very best as we walk along this journey together.

Wade Thomas
Phoenix, AZ
October 2020

CHAPTER 1:

THE MEANING OF HEART-BASED CULTURE

First things first, before a heart-based culture can be built we need to have a clear understanding of what it means and doesn't mean. A heart-based culture is one that features compassion and empathy. When we hear the words compassion and empathy we often think of soft, easy, accommodating. However, a culture focused on these things is not that at all. Heart based cultures still feature accountability and the necessity of making the tough decisions. It is an important distinction to make, as many leaders were brought up in an environment where words like compassion and empathy were something akin to weakness, traits that led to not achieving results and in turn failing.

The term compassion really describes a situation where a leader cares about others, selflessly helps others. Empathy speaks to a deep level of understanding and relation to other's thoughts, feelings and experiences. Notice the common denominator here, the use of the term others. Compassion and empathy in the context of a heart-based culture speak to a focus on others. The strength in this is that as the organization as a whole focuses on others, the entire organization becomes very compassionate, very empathetic, very healthy and very strong.

One more great thing to note about compassion and empathy is that they are not fixed traits. They can be learned. This is contrary to a common belief that compassion and empathy are like a person's height or eye color—fixed for life. Research shows, however, that compassion and empathy can improve with practice. When people are given time and support, they can develop and enhance the skills that it takes to be compassionate and empathetic.

Compassion and Empathy in Business

Today's business leaders generally recognize the importance of culture in their organizations, but many don't think about compassion and empathy as being an important part of it. After all, it's not always obvious in a competitive, bottom line driven environment to think in these terms. The pressures of today's business climate, with its fierce competition and disruption, often lead to the belief that the business needs a culture that creates a single-minded pursuit of financial objectives. This is reinforced by a management history of control focused leaders who are solely focused on driving productivity at any cost. This has been so prevalent throughout our history that it is well memorialized in business books, classes, and even pop culture. It is further reinforced by people's personal experiences, so many have endured working for organizational yellers, screamers and general bullies.

As a result of this, when we hear organizational culture described, we are more likely to hear terms such as accountability, pace, urgency, and results. But the reality is that compassion and empathy are not in opposition to these things, rather they enable them.

What does compassion and empathy look like in a business environment? Culture consists of two basic elements. First, it defines the values and beliefs of the organization. The values of a heart-based organization tend to include words such as integrity, respect, teamwork, caring, fairness, and inclusion. The second element of culture is that it guides the behaviors of the organization through shared assumptions and norms. In a heart-based culture, there is a belief that that everyone belongs to one team, one family and because of this the assumption is that others are capable and act in the best interest of the team. This belief in turn leads to a higher level of trust at all levels. Somebody looking at the organization from outside will notice higher levels of engagement, lower turnover and absenteeism, and a more content workforce.

Contrast this with organizations that have the opposite assumption, that have a belief system built around the assumption that people are untrustworthy and lazy, and whose values are centered around competition and control. These assumptions and values lead to an environment of distrust, with people focusing on individual accomplishments often at the expense of the team as a whole. A prime example of this type of culture is Enron, whose well known ruthless culture created enormous wealth for its executives (at the expense of those less powerful) but eventually led to its demise.

While Enron is certainly an extreme example, there are plenty of cultural elements in most businesses that lead to employee suffering. It can be day to day realities such as insensitive management, tough deadlines, unending schedules, unrealistic demands—the list goes on. It can also be event driven. Activities such as downsizing or restructuring, or changes in workload or processes, can also lead to pain for those affected. Heart driven organizations utilize compassion and empathy to ease the pain and suffering of their workforce.

The bottom-line truth is that the requirements for leadership have changed dramatically over the past decade or so. Historically managing a workforce was much more procedural. The work was much more predictable and routine, an environment that gave rise to command and control leadership. Managers were tasked with making sure that people performed the job that they were told to do, in the way that they were told to do it, and during the allotted timeframe. Things have changed. The average worker now changes jobs 10-15 times during their career. The workplace is more complex and ambiguous than in any time before. The pace of change, and indeed the work itself has increased dramatically. Employees today are required to have a much higher level of thought and decision making. In this work environment, the old command and control approach is no longer effective.

The people in an organization must become more thoughtful, collaborative and resourceful. This requires that companies care about their organizations and want to give their best. Companies must overcome the old way of doing things that has been so ingrained in leaders and must look at leadership (and their leaders) in a whole new way.

Throughout this book we will discuss the principals of a heart-based culture and how you can put these into practice in your organization. But first, in the next chapter, we will talk about the benefits of having a culture of compassion and empathy.

KEY TAKEAWAYS

Compassion and empathy enable organizational capabilities

In a heart-based culture, there is a belief that that everyone belongs to one team, one family and because of this the assumption is that others are capable and act in the best interest of the team. This belief in turn leads to a higher level of trust at all levels

There are plenty of cultural elements in most businesses that lead to employee suffering. Heart driven organizations utilize compassion and empathy to ease this pain for their workforce.

MAKE IT REAL

What are the values and beliefs in your organization?

What are some of the assumptions and norms?

CHAPTER 2:

BENEFITS OF A HEART-BASED CULTURE

There are many benefits of a heart-based culture. These benefits are deep reaching, spanning from the societal level, to personal, to business and organization level. This chapter addresses each of these levels and demonstrates the powerful effect compassion and empathy can have across the entire spectrum.

Benefits to Society

The benefits of a heart-based culture start at the society level. Now, more than ever, we need compassion and empathy. Society today is caught up in rampant individualism, with people seemingly focused inward on themselves more and more every day. Social norms are tossed aside seemingly every day as we become more and more self-interested. The irony is that people are at their core social creatures, we need and value community. This has never been more apparent than during our recent experience with the social isolation measures that came about with the Covid-19 breakout. In order to achieve the community that we as society value, it is necessary to engage with each other. And the engine for that engagement is compassion and empathy. Only through compassion and empathy can we productively work out our differences and heal the rifts that have developed in our society.

Benefits to the Individual

Compassion and empathy also have many benefits on the individual level. Using compassion and empathy increases your perspective and helps you understand that you have much more in common with others than you have differences, that others experience the ups and downs just as you do. Having compassion and empathy helps you become better connected and have deeper relationships with those around you. It has also been shown to improve health by strengthening the immune system, lowering stress, and normalizing blood pressure. In general, having compassion and empathy will make you a healthier, happier, better connected, and more fulfilled person.

There are also advantages when you use compassion and empathy in your organization. Interacting with our superiors, peers, and customers in a compassionate and empathetic way leads to increased positivity within our own lives. Further, studies show that leaders who exercise compassion and empathy are seen more favorably by employees and clients and are able to get greater engagement from both. These traits lead to increased opportunities for these leaders.

Benefits for Business

Every bit as significant as the societal and personal impact of having compassion and empathy is the impact that it can have on business. In the United States, an estimated 88 percent of the workforce, 130 million people, go home every day feeling that they work for an organization that doesn't listen to or care about them. This represents a huge opportunity for any organization to differentiate themselves.

While compassion and empathy are recognized in many different areas of our lives, they are not often thought of as being part of a business culture. But research now has made the connection between compassion, empathy, and business success. Compassion and empathy, when embedded into a heart-based culture, create positive outcomes throughout the organization.

Outcomes of a Heart-Based Culture

The research shows that in organizations that have a culture of compassion and empathy, employees experience reduced stress and higher job satisfaction. In this type of culture, people have the ability to vent to colleagues, supervisors, or anyone else in the organization. This serves to get stress off their chest which prevents it from building up inside. This helps even out the stress level and get people onto an even keel. They have less anxiety and are more resilient to challenging situations and to burnout. This leads to higher employee engagement, increased loyalty, and commitment to the organization. Furthermore, it leads to increased cooperation and teamwork throughout the business.

There is also a physical component to being in a heart-based culture. As mentioned earlier, studies on workplace health and well-being have indicated that a positive work environment leads to a steady blood pressure and heart rate and a stronger immune system. This leads to reduced absenteeism and less use of sick leave. Employees take this home as well, bringing positivity into their family and social life.

Implementing a heart-based culture also has an impact on organizational trust. When an organization has compassion and empathy, trust is created between the organization and its employees. Leaders who practice compassion and empathy have employees who are committed to putting their all into the company. They repay the actions of their leaders by putting forth great efforts to achieve organizational goals. They also form strong and highly effective professional relationships and collaborate freely with their colleagues.

Strategic Advantages

These outcomes create many advantages for the business. Heart-based cultures make strategic advantages more sustainable. There are five types of strategic advantage that are directly driven by a heart-based culture: attracting, retaining and engaging talented people, innovation, customer relations, adaptability, and collaboration.

- **Attracting, Retaining and engaging talented people.** Accomplishing great things as an organization requires a strong team. Finding them, keeping them, and engaging them is central to any strategic advantage. The rise of technology and social media has created a far more transparent environment than we have ever seen. While in the past it was difficult for a candidate to truly understand the inner working of an organization, now it is simply a matter of reading social media or looking at sites such as Glassdoor. Another large factor is the rise of the millennial generation in the workforce. Millennials are now the largest generation in the workforce, passing baby boomers. Their desires from an employer are much different. Recent surveys show that millennials are looking for a collaborative and innovative culture and leadership teams that are committed to employee success. Both of these areas are natural byproducts of a heart-based culture, and companies that successfully incorporate heart-based values will have a huge advantage in attracting talent.

  Employees in a heart-based culture are also likely to stay a long time, and while they are there will be more engaged in the business. They will feel a close affinity to the team, it will become like a family for them. A heart-based culture helps ensure that the organization will have the right people in place at the right time with the commitment to achieve their goals.

- **Innovation.** Whether it be breakthrough or disruptive

innovation, or basic process innovations, the ability of a business to continue moving forward and advancing its capabilities is a key component of success. A culture with compassion and empathy fosters psychological safety (more on that later), creating an environment where employees are motivated to learn, develop creative ideas, and take risks. The heart-based culture frees their minds to advance the business.

- **Customer Relations.** When compassion and empathy are delivered authentically with the customer, strong bonds are formed. A heart-based culture does not only impact employees, it also flows through to your customers. This builds long lasting customer loyalty and a strong brand. Think about the effectiveness the Nordstrom retail chain has had with bringing compassion and empathy to their customer experience. They have achieved a high level of recognition for how they relate to customers, and these customers are raving fans with intense brand loyalty.

- **Adaptability.** In today's fast-moving environment, adaptability and the ability to be nimble is a must have for organizations of all types. Compassion and empathy enable adaptability by reducing the negative emotional impacts of change and in turn lighting an interest to create positive change.

- **Collaboration.** Collaboration, when done well, dramatically improves an organizations ability to innovate, problem solve, and create optimal solutions. In a culture with compassion and empathy, people feel more comfortable sharing with their colleagues. They are not self-interested or afraid to share their input. The collaborative relationships that are fostered in this environment will lead to both the employees and the business to thrive.

Through these five components, a heart-based culture contributes to financial and operational resilience, customer acquisition and retention, and profitability. Because of its impact on these areas, and the resulting improvement in organizational capability, a heart-based culture creates a sustainable competitive advantage for the business and creates separation from its competition. In short, not only do compassion and empathy matter, but compassion and empathy win!

Now that we know the power of the heart-based culture to create competitive edge, the next section of the book discusses eight heart-based principles that will enable your business to start building the culture.

KEY TAKEAWAYS

Leaders who exercise compassion and empathy are seen more favorably by employees and clients and are able to get greater engagement from both.

In organizations that have a culture of compassion and empathy, employees experience reduced stress and higher job satisfaction This leads to higher employee engagement, increased loyalty, and commitment to the organization. Furthermore, it leads to increased cooperation and teamwork throughout the business.

When an organization has compassion and empathy, trust is created between the organization and its employees. Leaders who practice compassion and empathy have employees who are committed to putting their all into the company.

There are five types of strategic advantage that are directly driven by a heart-based culture: attracting, retaining and engaging talented people, innovation, customer relations, adaptability, and collaboration.

MAKE IT REAL

Which benefits to the individual resonate with you?

Rate your organization on a scale of 1-5 for each of the five types of strategic advantage. Where could you improve?

CHAPTER 3:

PRINCIPLE #1 – CREATE AN ENVIRONMENT FOR INDIVIDUAL SUCCESS

At the heart of creating a heart-based culture for the organization is to create an environment where individuals can succeed. One of the highest callings of any leader is to help their employees to be the best that they can be, and this is no different for the organization as a whole. This chapter covers steps that an organization, and its leaders, can take to create this environment.

Actively Seek Perspective

Think about the impact to a leader if they could understand fully what is going on with their employees. Imagine if they could walk in the shoes of their own leader, or their peers. What if each leader understood the pressures and trials that everyone around them is going through?

A large measure of compassion and empathy in a culture is how it deals with pain and suffering when it is experienced by its members. Pain and suffering can happen in the individual's personal life, and it can also happen in the workplace. In any organization there will be different viewpoints. Activities and decisions that may benefit the business as a whole often come at the detriment of some subset of the organization. These situations lead to a level of pain or suffering with the adversely impacted employees. A heart-based culture seeks to understand and to help ease the suffering and to help the individual through the difficult time—whether it be personal or business related.

The first part of developing compassion and empathy in these situations is to know that it exists. When suffering is not noticed, then there is no chance for it to be dealt with. While it seems like noticing the suffering would be an easy thing, it often is quite difficult. It requires someone, especially a leader, to be attuned to the emotions of the individuals on the team. If someone is paying attention, people often offer clues. This may take the form of an unusual lack of engagement. Sometimes their body language will show fatigue or tension. There might be anger or sadness on their face. The key to noticing and dealing with suffering at work is to pick up on these clues. When leaders notice these clues, they should be prompted to proactively seek more information. An example of an approach to this is "I can see that you are not quite yourself, it might help both of us if I could understand why".

The ability to notice suffering starts with the leader's

rapport with the people on their team. A leader in a heart-based culture has a hunger for learning more, a curiosity that goes far beyond asking how their day is going. They dig deep, they understand what makes each of their employee's tick—as individuals. They make themselves available and approachable. A leader who makes it easy for others to access them, and who is not afraid of personal issues, will find it a lot easy to notice and handle suffering in their team. This is also important from an organizational perspective. Businesses that have widespread cultural beliefs about putting on a good face or keeping our home problems at home make it harder to understand suffering.

Side Note

Don't be afraid to help employees with personal problems. Many of us came of age in our professional careers believing that work is work and home is home—nary shall the two meet. But the reality in today's world is work and home have become blended. With smartphones we are never far away from email, IM's, social media, and so on. Work follows us home, and home follows us to work. It is also unrealistic to leave your personal problems at home, just like it is unrealistic to not bring your work problems home. Going forward, successful, heart-based leaders must have a comfort level with being supportive of their employees even with personal issues.

It is important in a heart-based culture for leaders at all levels to immerse themselves in the daily grind from time to time. Part of this is understanding that no job is too low. One of the most effective ways to gain perspective is to spend some time walking in the shoes of others. There is a coffee shop near my house that recently changed ownership. The first time I went in I was met by the new owner. He then took my order and proceeded to make my coffee. As I sat there enjoying my coffee, I noticed that he was also cleaning machinery, washing dishes and cooking food—even though he had several employees working there at the time. He did this so that he could empathize with his people, understand where they were coming from and what issues they were confronted with. Which brings up another point, heart-based leaders lead from the front. They are there to support and guide their team, no matter how challenging the situation may be.

Seeking perspective is especially important and valuable during times of change. Having leaders who are attuned to the emotions of their team, and who notice suffering and can relate to it with empathy, make the change process more effective. A more formalized approach should also be taken when a significant change is about to occur. Inviting all stakeholders in to discuss their perspectives is a good technique to understand the multiple viewpoints that exist and to open the doorway to listening with empathy.

Many leaders have the ability to have a vision and communicate it. What separates the truly great leader is their ability to get their message to resonate with others. Seeking perspective with compassion and empathy creates an environment where there is a true connection between a leader and their employees, an environment where the employee knows that the leader is concerned about them. This connection adds weight and meaning to their words, allowing them to drive true success.

Heart-Based Culture in Action

Early in my career, I was a plant Human Resources Manager. After a period of dramatic underperformance and poor leadership, a new Plant Manager was introduced to the division. His first step was not to pour over the financials, huddle up with the leaders, or jump into massive change initiatives. Instead he tasked his senior leadership team with bringing their teams into his office to meet him. During this introduction, each senior leader was required to do more than the standard introduction by name, title, years of service, and so on. Instead, they were required to tell the Plant Manager, in their own words, things about them. Their interests, hobbies, career aspirations etc. As you might imagine, a few of the senior leaders had to scramble and learn as much as they could in a short period of time. The message the Plant Manager sent was a powerful one. The way we operate our business is that we know our people.

Create Psychological Safety

Too many of us have been exposed to bosses who lead by fear. Many have been exposed to entire cultures based on the belief that fear is the best way to motivate. This could not be further from the truth.

When people feel afraid how are they going to show up? When they are afraid, are they going to give their all? Or will they play it safe, avoiding risk for fear of losing their job or being embarrassed? In a fear based environment, people must play a defensive game. They hide themselves behind emotional masks, focused only on survival. This creates a problem for organizations. When employees are behind their protective masks, they also hide their engagement, creativity, trust and loyalty. Those traits are all heart-based and are severely limited in a fear-based culture.

A study by Dr. George Land and Dr. Beth Jarvis shows that when given tests to see how well they generated ideas, 98% of children at 5 years old scored at a genius level for creativity. Five years later, those same children had dropped down to 30%. By the time they got into high school, only 12% of them were still classified as highly creative. Even worse than that, when they studied 280,000 adults they found that only 2% of adults still have this genius-level creativity. What is happening here? As we grow up, we learn to put limits on ourselves. We are given boundaries almost from the time of birth, and this causes a subconscious desire to build walls, to stay within our lines, and to stay in our comfort zone.

People sacrifice creativity and self-expression for safety and protection from perceived risk.

This sacrifice is detrimental to the growth of an organization and the individuals within it. In order for organizations to reach their full potential, they must create a space that provides psychological safety. This is important for the long-term success of the people on the team. It should not be seen as an employee benefit or a tool to simply make employees happy, rather it is an imperative to the long-term success of an organization. Psychological safety speaks to an environment where people are willing to take risks and be vulnerable with each other. Where there is a willingness to discuss and learn from failures and mistakes.

Studies show that when employees feel safe to take risks, they strive to surpass their goals, are more open to feedback, help each other even outside of their own area, and use their creativity to solve problems. This safety also creates a higher willingness to admit and report failures. The result of this is that failures are identified, corrected, and avoided in the future. However, many organizations do the opposite. They make it dangerous to take risks, they punish failure and resort to discipline instead of constructive learning. This creates an environment where employees are afraid to report mistakes, and as a result organizational learning is limited and the mistakes are likely to be repeated over and over again. This environment also limits an employee's ability or willingness to communicate essential information about what is going on at the ground level of the business—information that is crucial to operating successfully.

Side Note

There are different types of failure and they must be handled differently:

- Learning failures. These failures occur as a result of sensible risk taking or experimentation. These types of failures have great learning value and should be encouraged. They drive the mission of the organization forward.
- Circumstantial failure. This type of failure is largely driven by circumstances that occur in a way they never have before—in such a way that they could not have been anticipated. While there are certainly opportunities to learn from these failures, they are generally not to be encouraged.
- Preventable failure. A failure that occurs as a result of not following procedures. These types of failures need to be addressed firmly and directly. People are generally knowledgeable enough to know that those who violate procedures are putting everyone at risk. In this case, addressing these failures with fair but firm responses increases psychological safety.

In order for an environment where employees feel psychologically safe to exist, there must be trust that the organization is looking out for their best interest. That trust is created from visible actions and communication, not simply from intent.

Leaders need to consciously look at failures from the lens of learning. Analyze what could have gone better and then look to implement changes. Moving to a learning phase quickly after a failure is crucial to creating psychological safety.

Remove Barriers

An important function of organizations and their leaders is to help foster their employees' success by removing barriers. A strong, heart-based leaver never stops asking questions or getting feedback. These inquiries allow leaders to keep a pulse on what gets in the way of their team's success. Staying ahead of the curve allows leaders to proactively support their team by clearing the path for them by helping redefine processes, remove bureaucracy, and get past bottlenecks.

This involvement goes beyond the direct leadership. A heart-based organization gets everybody involved in removing barriers. Quite often the people that can help remove barriers are not the direct leaders. They might be senior executives, or they can be lower level employees in different departments. The key is that everybody is focused on understanding the issues and working to resolve them.

The previous paragraphs discussed barriers that are very tangible. But there are other barriers that are just as real. In many cases, people are held back by mindset. Leaders in a heart-based organization are able to understand and be in tune with the emotions of the people who work for them. They can understand what emotions and mindsets hold the employee back, and which propel them to success. The objective of the leader is to help their employee leverage the positive mindsets and to help them work through negative mindsets and encourage new patterns of thinking.

Heart-Based Culture in Action

I once worked with a senior executive who was responsible for a substantial number of business units across a large geography. Despite this, he made it a point to travel to each of his business units at least twice a year. During his trips, he met with not only the business unit leadership teams, but also with rank and file employees. His mission was to get an idea for what the issues were in the individual markets. This provided him with insights on what the teams needed and what resources he needed to deploy to help ensure their success.

Emphasize Growth

One of the most powerful advantages of a heart-based culture is that it focuses on growth. Growth at the individual level leads to growth at the enterprise level. A culture of compassion and empathy is not only interested in motivating employees to increase company profitability, but also in helping them grow on an individual level. This long-term outlook in turn helps the company sustain their competitive advantage and profitability over time.

Individual growth starts with standards. A heart-based organization has high standards, both for itself and for the people that work there. It might sound counterintuitive for some that compassion and high standards go together, but they do. People tend to strive for the standards that are set for them. By setting standards that are too low you are doing a disservice, because many people will stop once they have achieved the standards. They will stop growing and will fall short of their potential. Heart-based leaders don't just have high standards and watch from afar, however. They will create an environment where their employees will strive to grow, and the leader will be right there to support them as they stretch.

Another contributing factor to employee growth is how organizations make decisions. Often, they look at decisions as a dichotomy: either they make a decision for the benefit of the business or for the benefit of the person. As a result, decisions are made for the perceived benefit of the business that are detrimental to the individual. A common example of this is a situation where there is a job opening with two candidates. Candidate A is from the outside, has a wealth of experience and success in the role being hired for, and knows what they are doing. Candidate B is an internal candidate, an up and comer in the business, has supported the role in question but has never done it directly. The safe play, and one often taken, is to hire candidate A. They have done the job (albeit with a different company, culture, and context) and have a great track record. However, a heart-based organization will take an approach that helps team members grow in a way that also positively impacts the business. This organization would take the risk on Candidate B, knowing that over time these decisions will have a very large, cumulatively positive result on the business.

One very persistent source of suffering in the workplace is lack of advancement or the boredom that sets in after long periods in the same job. A heart-based organization is in tune with this suffering and can take steps to alleviate it through creative role design, additional training, and development planning.

Heart-Based Culture in Action

My very first job after obtaining my MBA was as a Human Resources Representative in the Compensation and Benefits department of a large company. The plan was for me to work in the corporate office for a few years, gaining experience before being sent off to run Human Resources for a business unit. After six months, a Human Resource Manager position opened up suddenly in a struggling 400 employee union plant. The traditional hiring pattern at the company was to hire experienced Human Resources professionals into those roles, and in fact there were several readily available within the company and externally. But the company made the decision to take the chance on my growth and provide me the opportunity. This decision process was duplicated with four other senior positions in the plant, with up and comers given the opportunity to grow over the safe decision of hiring seasoned managers. A little over a year later the plant turned its first profit in its history. The decisions to choose the growth

of the employee over the safe business decision yielded
a result that was a rousing success for both the business
and the individuals.

Provide Encouragement and Support

Some of the most common forms of organizational suffering
reported by employees are lack of appreciation for their talents and skills, of working for supervisors who didn't understand the difficulties of their work, and of feeling like their
work is not meaningful. These forms of suffering are often
deeply rooted and are often taken for granted as just the
way things are. An organization that is heart-based purpose-
fully addresses each of these forms of suffering by providing
encouragement and support.

Verbal encouragement goes a long way in demonstrating
compassion and empathy. Organizations and leaders can
demonstrate their appreciation by continually supporting
and cheering others for their hard work, their talent, and
their achievements. This can be a challenge for many leaders
because its often difficult to see the effects of the encouragement right away, but it's important to keep up the support
because they may never know when their words will hit home
and bring about favorable changes, but they no doubt will.

It is also important for heart-based leaders to be solution-focused. Exploring the causes of underachievement and
failures, and relying on employing resources to solve the issue
rather than being overly critical on mistakes goes a long way
toward easing the suffering that occurs with failure.

Helping employees find meaning in their work is also important in the heart-based culture. Organizations should regularly articulate their mission, vision, strategy and goals. Individual leaders can then provide context to the employee on how their everyday work helps the organization fulfill their mission, vision, strategy, and goals. Every person needs to feel the sense that what they do matters, they want to feel pride in their work. Organizations can take this a step further by connecting their activities with how they contribute to society. One company that I worked for built new homes. Their slogan "Building the American Dream" was a continual reminder of how the organization, and its employees, contributed to society as a whole and created meaning for everyone involved.

Understand Team Dynamics

Team dynamics make a significant difference in a heart-based culture. When you think about it, people spend most of their work time with their team. With this in mind it is obvious that the quality of interpersonal connections between people plays a substantial role in the effectiveness of any culture. High quality connections are characterized by the feelings of mutuality, alignment and positive regard that occur during interactions, no matter how brief. These high-quality connections have powerful implications in a heart-based culture. They create an environment where colleagues can express both negative emotions and positive emotions without risking the relationship. For example, a colleague can express dissatisfaction with someone who misses a deadline and at the same time express positive concern or care about the reasons for missing the deadline. This has a very positive effect on the flow of communication and the resolution of problems because people can rely on the mutual respect and trust that has been built up.

High quality connections also mean that colleagues will often notice different things about one another that the leader may not pick up on. Earlier in this chapter we discussed the need for leaders to be attuned to the emotions of their employees. A high-quality team can distribute this emotional awareness across multiple people, providing a higher level of information to the leader.

Another important element of team dynamics is the way that the leader interacts with the team and what role they play. An empathetic leader feels the vibrations of the team, understands their ebbs and flows, and knows when to step in and take the lead and when to let the team run. A great heart-based leader will step back and let the team run when things are going well so that the team can feel the win. They are like the centerpiece of a room, they provide a focal point but are not directly involved in what happens in the room, they are not the center of attention.

Conversely, the leader should jump in in times where there is danger of catastrophic failure. Keep in mind that failure can be a good thing, and a leader should allow his team the opportunity to fail in some things so that they learn the lesson, but if there is danger of a major, damaging failure a strong leader will jump in.

Heart-Based Culture in Action

I have had a client for many years who has mastered the ability to feel the team. He is responsible for a very large business unit of a multi-billion-dollar company. He is very visible and supportive with his team, but he lets them do their thing. He trusts in their abilities and understands that they were hired to do a job—and he let's them do that. He provides ongoing encouragement and works to remove the barriers and obstacles that get in their way, but otherwise the wins and losses are theirs. However, when something major does happen, he is quick to jump into the lead and direct the team. In these times, even though his team is used to taking the lead themselves, they look to him for guidance. This is a result of the mutual trust that has been built up as a result of this leader understanding the dynamics of his team.

KEY TAKEAWAYS

A heart-based culture seeks to understand and to help ease the suffering and to help the individual through difficult times—whether it be personal or business related.

It is important in a heart-based culture for leaders at all levels to immerse themselves in the daily grind from time to time.

Creating a space that provides psychological safety is important for the long-term success of the people on the team. Psychological safety speaks to an environment where people are willing to take risks and be vulnerable with each other. Where there is a willingness to discuss and learn from failures and mistakes.

An important function of organizations and their leaders is to help foster their employees' success by removing barriers.

The objective of the leader is to help their employee leverage the positive mindsets and to help them work through negative mindsets and encourage new patterns of thinking.

Individual growth starts with standards. A heart-based organization has high standards, both for itself and for the people that work there.

A heart-based organization will take an approach that helps team members grow in a way that also positively impacts the business.

It is important for heart-based leaders to be solution-focused. Exploring the causes of underachievement and failures, and relying on employing resources to solve the issue rather than being overly critical on mistakes goes a long way toward easing the suffering that occurs with failure.

Verbal encouragement goes a long way in demonstrating

compassion and empathy.

Helping employees find meaning in their work is important in the heart-based culture. Organizations should regularly articulate their mission, vision, strategy and goals. Individual leaders can then provide context to the employee on how their everyday work helps the organization fulfill their mission, vision, strategy, and goals.

High quality connections are characterized by the feelings of mutuality, alignment and positive regard that occur during interactions, no matter how brief. These high-quality connections have powerful implications in a heart-based culture. They create an environment where colleagues can express both negative emotions and positive emotions without risking the relationship.

An empathetic leader feels the vibrations of the team, understands their ebbs and flows, and knows when to step in and take the lead and when to let the team run.

MAKE IT REAL

Ask your leaders how each of their employees are doing, not on a superficial level, but on a deeper level. If they struggle with this, help them come up with a plan to learn the perspectives of the people who work for them.

Develop a program where leaders rotate through lower level jobs in the organization. Ask them to report on their findings to the leadership team. Develop a list of actions that can be taken to remove barriers for or improve the work life in those jobs.

Develop a process for handling failure and train your leaders in it. Publicly celebrate the learnings from learning failures.

Review the standards that exist in the organization, raise the bar on standards that are low or have slipped. Celebrate the achievement of high standards.

Take a chance on a high potential employee. Provide them greater responsibility and visibility in the organization.

Put a focus on recognizing employee achievements. Encourage your leaders to recognize and appreciate their employees regularly.

CHAPTER 4:

PRINCIPLE #2 – MAKE THE HARD DECISIONS

There are times in any business where hard decisions must be made. A heart-based organization is no different, and in fact a hard decision is often the compassionate thing to do. This might seem counterintuitive, but the reality is that much suffering is created when someone is working in a job that they are unable to be successful in. People don't like to perform jobs where they fail over and over again, where they don't have the ability to succeed. It's not a healthy experience. Another side of this is the effect an underperforming employee has on the rest of the team, often creating frustration, resentment, and other pain. Throughout my career I have seen many occasions where the hard decision was put off, often due to misled attempts at compassion. In these occasions organizations and leaders chose to allow the poorly performing employee to flame out and leave on their own accord. While this may feel like the easy way out, the damage done during the process to both the employee and the team is very detrimental and often requires a great deal of repair.

Another thing that often gets in the way is the perception that hard decisions aren't fair, that everyone should be equal regardless of talent or performance. The truth is, there is a lot of attention given to leaders being "unfair" in this time of "participation trophies". This again creates an environment where leaders avoid the decisions that separate strong performers from poor performers. The reality is that this type of behavior is inherently unfair. It's unfair to the high performers who aren't recognized for their contributions, and it's unfair to the lower performers who are allowed to flounder in positions that they are unsuccessful in. It is at the core of a leader's job to make the distinctions in performance, and make the hard decisions that go along with it.

The important thing, and often an area that separates a heart-based culture from others, is how the hard decision is handled. Too often I have seen (as I am sure many others have seen) the process of making and communicating these decisions to be dictated by policies and legal protocols. The decision and communication being dictated by high risk avoidance at the cost of compassion and empathy. While certainly there is some overlap between the two, too often we see these activities handled in a cold and unfeeling manner.

Side Note
Some questions to ask to help determine if the situation

can be salvaged.
- Does the employee have the skills, abilities, and mindset to perform the job?
- Is the shortfall in part of their job or all of their job?
- Are they high performers in other aspects of their job?
- Is the poor performance a new development?
- Are their circumstantial factors that could be causing the low performance? For example, something in their personal life.
- Does the underperformance seem temporary, or more long-lasting?
- What is the likelihood that the performance can be improved within a reasonable timeframe?

A heart-based culture will handle these situations with a focus on compassion. The key elements of this approach are:

Minimize Surprises. Issues should be addressed as they arise. In almost all cases, the performance issue did not arise overnight. Leaders should engage with the employee as soon as the situation begins. The quicker the intervention, the more chance that the employee has to course correct and make the improvement needed. These conversations are another area where policy often trumps compassion. Managers often get wrapped around the documentation aspect. They build Disciplinary Actions, Performance Improvement Plans, and Final Warnings around the assumption that the employee will fail and that these documents will be used in some anticipated or imagined litigation someday. The idea that the leader can actually help the employee turn around is often an afterthought at best.

A heart-based culture takes this approach and turns it around. While documentation is still important, the purpose of the leader's intervention is to let the employee know that there is a problem and to help them improve. Part of this is intervening quickly when a problem arises. Catching it in the early stages can often lead to a quick resolution. If a Disciplinary Action or Performance Improvement Plan is the first step, then it is already late. Using compassion and empathy in these interventions is important. A leader should strive to understand what is driving the underperformance and help remove any barriers that exist. A heart-based leader goes into this with the assumption that the employee generally wants to do a good job, that they aren't lazy or willful in their performance deficiency.

The idea of not having surprises is relevant for other types of terminations also. Often, we need to make these hard decisions not because of performance, but as a result of a reduction in force or a reorganization. A heart-based organization will be as transparent as possible when it comes to company performance and outlook. If the business isn't performing or the market is in decline, employees will know it long before reductions are necessary. While this will probably not eliminate suffering altogether, it will ease the pain somewhat as the impacted employee will have known the possibility existed and will have a higher level of understanding when it arrives.

Communicate the decision with compassion and empathy. Whether it be as a result of underperformance, or as a result of a reduction in force or reorganization, the way the decision is communicated is crucial. This is where heart-based organizations have compassionate conversations to explain the decision rather than hide behind legal concerns.

A client shared with me a reduction in force that he had participated in prior to our engagement. On the day it happened, human resources employees pulled the staff into two separate meetings. In one meeting, employees were told that the reduction was occurring but that they were not impacted. They were then sent back to work. In the other meeting, employees were told that they were being released and were then escorted out of the building with the instructions that their personal belongings would be shipped to the home address on file.

As you can imagine, the impact of this approach was less than positive. The employees who were still with the organization lost a lot of faith and trust in the organization, including many of their leaders. Productivity and engagement dropped significantly in the months that followed, and the results that led to the reduction continued to slide. The lack of compassion in this type of downsizing practice makes the financial suffering worse by adding emotional costs. The employee that has been released in this manner will tend to feel anger, resentment and other unproductive emotions. These emotions can lead to problems, legal and otherwise, for the company down the road.

It doesn't have to be that way. Adding compassion to the process can make a significant difference in people's emotional outcomes. Leaders who meet personally with those who are leaving and who express compassion for their circumstances reduce the suffering. Likewise, managers who address the pain and suffering with those who remain, and who allow for discussion of the events and what happened, encourage compassion. This compassion alleviates some of the pain associated with being a survivor, pain such as regret, remorse, and the stress of the increased workload that comes from the reduced workforce.

Be fair and generous. Heart-based organizations recognize the financial strain that is put on those that are let go, in particular due to reductions in force. One of the largest sources of suffering for impacted employees is the loss of income and the associated financial worries. This often gets in the way of their ability to bounce back and move forward. A compassionate and empathetic organization will be fair and generous with severance payments and other considerations, such as medical coverage and vacation payout. This not only helps the impacted employee move on, but it also has an effect on the remaining employees. While most companies do not publicly communicate how these situations are handled for most employees, word still gets out. Survivors who see the company act in a fair and generous manner, and who see the compassion and empathy behind it, will tend to trust the organization and better understand that the hard decision had to happen. Allowing employees to exit the organization with dignity and grace sends a message to the remaining employees that the company has their best interests at heart.

Heart-Based Culture in Action

Earlier in my career I led the human resources department for a large business unit. This business unit was originally a startup business that had grown significantly over a period of a few years. One member of the original team was still there after the significant growth. Unfortunately, the business had outgrown her. She struggled with the new demands and the faster pace of the larger business. It was a very difficult decision for all involved as she had been a key part of the startup. But it was a decision that we had to make. When it came time to have the conversation with her, the President of the organization met with her personally. He thanked her for all the great things she accomplished during her tenure, and acknowledged the role that she played in building the business. She was given a generous severance package and a commitment from both of us that we would help her in future endeavors as she needed. After we had finished informing her, the weight of the world seemed to fall off of her shoulders. She thanked us for all of the opportunities that had been provided for her and shared with us that she had been miserable struggling with the new business. She left the organization and quickly found a position in a smaller business that suited her much better.

KEY TAKEAWAYS

There are times in any business where hard decisions must be made. A heart-based organization is no different, and in fact a hard decision is often the compassionate thing to do.

Hard decisions should not come as a surprise to those impacted. Leaders should engage with the employee as soon as the situation begins. The quicker the intervention, the more chance that the employee has to course correct and make the improvement needed.

Adding compassion to the process when a hard decision must be communicated can make a significant difference in people's emotional outcomes.

A compassionate and empathetic organization will be fair and generous with severance payments and other considerations, such as medical coverage and vacation payout. This not only helps the impacted employee move on, but it also has a positive effect on the remaining employees.

MAKE IT REAL

Ask your leaders to evaluate each of their employees relative to the job they are performing. Challenge these evaluations, if they say an employee is doing "ok" or "satisfactory" ask they how they came to that conclusion. Ask how things would look if they had a different employee in that role.

If a leader struggles with an underperforming employee,

ask them to walk in that employee's shoes. How does that employee feel? What do they think of their lack of success? How would they feel in a job that was a better fit?

Train your leaders in how to deliver the hard news. Do not focus on process. Rather, focus on understanding the recipients thoughts and feelings and how to handle them.

Ensure that your organization is fair and generous in severance payments and is focused on helping employee's move on to the next chapter in their career.

CHAPTER 5:

PRINCIPLE #3 – INFLUENCE OVER AUTHORITY

In a business, influence is often confused with hierarchy or authority. In today's world they are two distinctly different things. Influence is the skill that one applies to bring others to their way of thinking. Authority is used to give direction. While authority and giving direction sound like the core of what leaders do, the reality is that authority relies on employees' acceptance of the direction. There may have been a time and a place when this was a given, but it is not generally the case today.

A heart-based organization understands this dynamic and welcomes it. In this type of environment leaders, colleagues, and employees treat each other with respect no matter what titles they may have. They work together and are open to discussion and assistance on anything that might arise. The primary focus of a heart-based leader in this environment is to influence not to dictate. Leaders are people that others want to follow, as opposed to having to follow. They get things done by earning trust, not through their position. This culture brings several benefits. One benefit is that employees who decide to follow their leader because of their influence will engage at a much deeper level than those that simply follow orders. Another benefit stems from the culture that emerges from this type of environment. When employees work together as a team, rather than a hierarchy, they open communication and problem-solving avenues that greatly enhance an organizations nimbleness and speed. Another great advantage of the heart-based approach is that it brings higher levels of meaning and engagement to the team. People feel good about their situation when they are working as a team as opposed to a hierarchy.

For these reasons, as an organization you want your leaders to leverage influence rather than lean on the crutch of authority. Some leaders find that this comes naturally but others, especially new leaders, are not accustomed to this approach. Much of gaining influence will happen as a natural byproduct of becoming immersed in a heart-based culture. The relationship building that will naturally happen during the process discussed in this book will predispose employees to want to follow the leader. They can further cement this influence by adopting four key influence mindsets. These mindsets are leading with vision, believing in your people, encouraging versus demanding, and guiding, acknowledging and supporting.

Lead with vision and character

An important mindset for developing influence is to lead with vision. It's important for leaders at all levels to be able to paint the picture, to speak to what their vision is for their span of control. Even front-line supervisors can benefit from this. People rally around ideas and challenges, especially when there is a focus. A leader can harness the energy that comes from this excitement to drive results. Just as important is to lead with character and integrity. Being seen as a leader who will do what's right, no matter how difficult, will greatly enhance influence and effectiveness.

Believe in your people

One of the greatest sources of empowerment is to simply believe in your people. The power of communicating this belief, looking at them and sincerely saying "I believe in you" goes a long way to developing the trust of your team. Giving trust will lead to earning trust, and this in turn will lead to greater influence for the leader.

Encourage versus demand

Even though we have all watched television shows depicting demanding bosses, and many of us have experienced them firsthand, the truth is that demanding will only work for so long. True leaders inspire their people to action. One thing that is true about every inspirational leader is that they leverage encouragement heavily. The reason for this is that encouragement is a powerful tool for leading people.

Encouragement is more than cheerleading or just saying "Good Job!". Encouragement is letting people know that they are trusted in their abilities, that their leader is confident that they can accomplish great things. Leaders can demonstrate their trust by giving their employees more responsibilities, and by providing positive feedback as they accomplish these responsibilities. Encouragement is also showing compassion and empathizing with employees. People will follow leaders when they feel that they truly care and have their best interests at heart. Demonstrating this compassion and showing that the leader is truly invested in the employee's wellbeing will increase the influence and commitment.

Guide, acknowledge and support

Influential leaders find a purpose in bettering the lives of others. Their goal is to help people reach their potential, knowing that the results will follow. They measure themselves by the growth and development of the people that they lead. A leader can greatly enhance their influence by helping people on their team discover and use their own unique powers, their own talents. They provide guidance and support and realize that given that environment their people will make great things happen. A great way to start this is to provide their people with opportunities for wins. Providing opportunities to overcome challenges, no matter how small, will help people stretch. In turn, this stretching will lead people to respect the leader who helped them with these wins.

As you finish this chapter, I challenge you to think about your leaders. Ask one question about each of the leaders: "Would their team respect and follow them if they had all has the same title?" If the answer is "yes", then you have a leader!

Heart-based Culture in Action

An organization that I worked with suffered the loss of a senior executive. At the time there were four leaders underneath the senior executive. For a number of reasons, the company decided not to name a replacement for the departing executive. The four leaders continued to operate within their spheres but with no direct reporting relationship to an executive. During this time one of the four emerged as a de facto leader of the group. This leader was well known for helping people develop their skills, was very supportive and encouraging, and had developed a strong relationship with each of the other three. The other three easily deferred to him, despite the fact that they all had the same title. The organization did not miss a beat, and eventually the leader was given the official title.

KEY TAKEAWAYS

The primary focus of a heart-based leader in this environment is to influence not to dictate. They get things done by earning trust, not through their position.

There are four key influence mindsets. These mindsets are leading with vision and character, believing in your people, encouraging versus demanding, and guiding, acknowledging and supporting.

A leader can greatly enhance their influence by helping people on their team discover and use their own unique powers, their own talents.

MAKE IT REAL

Ask one question about each of the leaders: "Would their team respect and follow them if they had all has the same title?" If the answer is "yes", then you have a leader!

CHAPTER 6:

PRINCIPLE #4 – DO NOT TOLERATE NEGATIVE BEHAVIOR

It is said that an organization is defined by its worst behavior. This is especially true if it is allowed to continue repeatedly. Think about how your organization responds to poor behavior. Is the behavior understood and addressed? Or is it ignored and dismissed? If you're in a position of leadership, people will view your response, good or bad, as indicative of your organizational culture.

Sometimes having a culture of compassion and empathy requires the courage to speak honestly about what is unacceptable. Sometimes it means taking a stand against inappropriate and negative behavior and taking definitive action to end the behavior.

Understand the Pulse

We have discussed how important it can be that the ties between people in an organization's networks are high quality and marked by respect and trust. But often networks have the opposite effect, creating rifts within the organization or placing people in corrosive relationships full of toxicity and negative energy. These networks can cause incalculable damage to a heart-based culture and must be eradicated quickly and decisively.

Heart-based leaders maintain a constant awareness of their team and work to prevent patterns of negative behavior from becoming the norm. There are many signs of negative behavior. It may be as obvious as turnover or absenteeism, but it can also be more indirect. Leaders might notice an employee who is avoided by others, a downturn in productivity in a group, or generally low morale.

When heart-based leaders identify these trends, they follow an important rule: they do not accept behavior that negatively impacts the team. Examples of this behavior include finger-pointing, not meeting deadlines that cause problems for others, gossiping, undermining, etc. These leaders do not wait until an issue arises through a complaint and then engage in conflict-resolution. Rather, they monitor behavioral patterns and seek to dismantle an issue before it rises to the level of a conflict.

Understanding the pulse and being out ahead of behavioral issues puts the leader in the position of not having to base decisions on the statements of a couple of people. It also creates trust in the team, they will develop confidence that their concerns will not be taken lightly.

Stop Negative Behavior Patterns

Negative behavior patterns can cause a lot of pain and suffering within the organization. What might start as relatively minor behaviors, as mentioned above, can grow into much larger issues. Patterns such as broken trust, caustic politics, manipulation, disrespect, toxic interactions or continual poor performance can create deep divides within an organization if left unaddressed. An organization that allows these behaviors in fact perpetuates them. Rather than allow the bad behavior patterns to grow exponentially, they must be dealt with strongly and with intense compassion. Intense compassion involves refusing to allow continued suffering in the workplace. This may involve everything from standing up to negative behavior to letting people go.

This becomes challenging when the person causing the negative behavior patterns is a high performer. It is not uncommon to hear statements like "he may be a bully, but he does excellent work" or "she may be difficult to work with, but she gets great numbers". Many organizations and leaders will turn a blind eye to negative behavior patterns that are created by high performers, because they are afraid of losing the performance. Heart-based cultures, however, follow a golden rule: High performance does not trump toxicity. An organization that has a true culture of compassion and empathy does not allow high performers to follow a different set of rules. They must live up to the same standards of behavior as everyone else.

Heart-based Culture in Action

I used to work with a sales leader who was a great illustration of high performance does not trump toxicity. Whenever he encountered a toxic salesperson who was also a top performer, he would address the issue and make the hard decision, even though it might cause a slip in sales. But what he found out is that, while he lost the high sales from the toxic salesperson the performance of the rest of the team increased by a factor even higher than the sales lost. His overall performance increased. This was not a one-off situation. During our time working together, I saw this pattern repeat itself over and over again, with the same results. This guiding principle of not accepting bad behavior patterns led not only to higher employee satisfaction, but also to better performance.

KEY TAKEAWAYS

Sometimes having a culture of compassion and empathy requires the courage to speak honestly about what is unacceptable. Sometimes it means taking a stand against inappropriate and negative behavior and taking definitive action to end the behavior.

Heart-based leaders maintain a constant awareness of their team and work to prevent patterns of negative behavior from becoming the norm.

Negative behavior patterns can cause a lot of pain and suffering within the organization. Patterns such as broken trust, caustic politics, manipulation, disrespect, toxic interactions or continual poor performance can create deep divides within an organization if left unaddressed. These patterns must be dealt with strongly with intense compassion.

Heart-based cultures, however, follow a golden rule: High performance does not trump toxicity.

MAKE IT REAL

Have a regular dialog with your leaders about their team, ask them specific questions around the individuals. Watch for key warning signs like avoidance or drops of productivity.

When you see high turnover or absenteeism in a particular work area, do a deep dive into that area. Don't settle for the superficial answer, dig deeper and find the root cause of the turnover.

Help your leaders get comfortable with dealing with toxic high performers, coach them to step up to the issues.

CHAPTER 7:

PRINCIPLE #5 – COMMUNICATE WITH COMPASSION AND EMPATHY

Communication plays a large role in any culture, and a heart-based culture is no different. In fact, research has shown that communicating with compassion and empathy improves the value system of the employees and they feel more involved with the organization. This chapter discusses the many elements of heart-based communication.

Environment

It is important to lay the groundwork to have a truly compassionate and empathetic communication system. The goal of communication in a heart-based culture is to create a dialogue between the organization and its employees to communicate organizational objectives, employee input and feelings, and other two-way feedback.

The first step in creating an environment where compassionate and empathetic communication can happen is to be transparent. Organizations often make the mistake of not sharing information openly. This can lead to distrust and a lack of confidence in having a dialogue. Organizations should share as much information as they can including customer feedback, data, target, strategies, etc.

Equally as important as organizational transparency is leadership authenticity. Leaders who desire to build empathy with their team must be willing to open themselves up, to be transparent, to show others their true person. Having compassion and empathy is a two-way street, it requires emotional engagement from both parties. This can often be a challenge, as authenticity requires some level of vulnerability, but it can be a true differentiator for a leader and an organization. In short, authenticity really matters.

Creating a space where leaders can be vulnerable will open many doors to authenticity and to true compassion and empathy. Organizations can accomplish this by encouraging open sharing without judgement. A heart-based organization must proactively eliminate stigmas that are often attached to the sharing of feelings and must act to prevent defensiveness or even retaliation when constructive criticism is offered. Feelings of shame or fear can easily lead people to withhold information, which in turn inhibits open communication and limits the organizations ability to respond with compassion and empathy.

Be Available and Present

Building compassionate and empathetic connections with others in the organization requires leaders to be present in both a physical and a psychological sense. Surveys show that employees check out when their leaders aren't present psychologically. They stop engaging, they limit their idea sharing, and they stop caring about the organization. Being present is crucial to prevent these outcomes.

Leaders can prevent this by keeping doors open, walking around the office regularly and eating meals in the kitchen or break room are great ways to make connections and engage with people at all levels. While being physically present seems like a relatively simple thing, it takes a conscious effort. It is easy for leaders to fall into a routine, to be caught up in their daily responsibilities and not take the time out to be available. It is important for them to put a focus on being available, on being present. A heart-based leader must consciously put aside the daily grind and make themselves available.

Psychological presence is also important. Leaders who demonstrate psychological presence will command loyalty and commitment. Being psychologically present means being in the moment, focusing on the person in front of them. They must put down the cell phone, look away from the laptop, shut down the email. Doing these things visibly itself sends a powerful message of interest. Other indicators of psychological presence include posture, body language, eye contact and asking questions. The effect of physical and psychological presence is that lines of communication will open, and the team will gain a feeling of psychological safety, which in turn will allow them to feel more comfortable sharing their thoughts and feelings.

Heart-based Culture in Action

I worked in the corporate office of a large company. The chief operating officer of the company, the second in command, was well known for greeting everybody as he walked into the office. He spent time every day walking around the office, talking to everybody he saw regardless of title. This kept him aware of what was going on with people, both personally and professionally. He became very approachable as a result of this, which led to him being a very well-respected leader in the organization, and in tune with the team. He demonstrated physical and psychological presence on a daily basis.

Active Inquiry

Two of the most powerful traits of heart-based leaders is a humble nature and the ability to listen. Leaders who exhibit these traits set themselves up to have compassionate and empathetic communication, and in turn will develop a strong rapport with the individuals on their team. These leaders learn to be persistently curious and strive to learn about the people who work for them, especially when it comes to challenges and difficulties that they are facing. This allows them to better understand the challenges faced by their team and the reasons behind the outcomes that they achieve (or don't achieve).

This curiosity, or active inquiry as I like to call it, helps leaders truly understand what an employee is going through. Active inquiry requires an openness to asking questions about what somebody is experiencing, rather than assume that their experience is the same as the leader's. There is a learnable technique to active inquiry. Active inquiry involves listening with the ears, eyes, and heart.

Leaders throughout the organization should develop the comfort and the language to ask humble, kind questions about someone's experience. They should observe the non-verbal clues that people give off to better understand. Active inquiry should be conducted in a no judgement zone. The purpose is to learn and encourage, as opposed to immediately solve or diminish. It is important for leaders to focus on listening in this phase, and to avoid the temptation to jump in with advice. They should seek to fully understand. The goal when listening is to identify patterns, only after the patterns are understood can quality feedback be provided.

Be Comfortable with the Personal Side

Lines between work and personal life have become more and more blurred, reaching a point that there is often no separation at all. Compassionate and empathetic leaders understand that their employees are complex individuals who are dealing with personal issues while maintaining their responsibilities at work. These leaders recognize that it's part of their role to lead and support those employees when they need it most, whether it is work-related or personal. This runs contrary to much of the conventional wisdom of the past decades, but the fact of the matter is that business and personal have become blended, and the thought that a leader should try and isolate this naturally occurring state is in conflict with the reality of life in today's world. How can a leader be compassionate, empathetic, and effective if they ignore half of what is going on with the people whom they lead?

I'm not suggesting that leader's become counselors or therapists, but rather that they show compassion and empathy in the face of their employee's suffering. A key component of a heart-based culture is the ability and willingness to show compassion when other people disclose a personal loss. This applies throughout the organization. Real connections and friendships at work are an important part of an employee's support structure. Compassion and empathy help leaders establish deep connections with those whom they are privileged to lead. The leader does not need to provide counseling for, nor do they even need to have personally experienced the suffering that their employee is going through. We all have experienced some form of suffering in our lives, the important thing is to empathize with the suffering employee and demonstrate compassion.

Heart-based Culture in Action

My father passed away from a heart attack in 2009. I spent the better part of two weeks in the hospital with him while they tried to save him. During these two weeks, I received a number of phone calls from supportive coworkers all around the country. The day that he finally passed away, I was working in the office. I received the news via telephone and stayed in the office not sure what to do. My leader, the CEO of the company, found out about it and came to my office. After spending some time sharing his own experiences with his father's passing, he eventually told me to go home so that I can have time to process. The compassion and empathy shown to me throughout all levels of that organization played a significant role in my processing of the pain and suffering of my father's passing. It is something that has stuck with me all these years.

Recognize All Levels

An interesting cause of workplace suffering is when an employee feels ignored or overlooked. Many organizations, perhaps subconsciously, treat low level employees as invisible. A heart-based organization must consciously make efforts to extend their compassion and empathy not just to high level employees and professionals, but also to those who make the copies or perform janitorial services. Flowers and cards and other sympathetic or celebratory measures are often seen in offices, but much less likely to be seen in mail rooms and janitorial closets. Recognizing these groups of employees goes a long way toward creating a heart-based culture that flows through the organization. It is important for a business to ensure that compassion and empathy reaches every nook and cranny of the organization.

Communicate Big Events with Compassion and Empathy

We discussed earlier the importance of carefully managing communications during reductions in force, but there are other big events that happen in the organization that can create pain and suffering. Events such as reorganizations, changes in leadership, and office moves are often more impactful to people than leaders realize. There are five steps that help communicate big events with compassion and empathy.

Pay attention to timing. The timing of the communication is often important. Announcing a big change on a Friday, for example, gives a lot of time over a weekend for an employee to attempt to process. Often this is without having the benefit of a lot of information or access to other co-workers. Having to stew over a major change alone for days can be a painful experience.

Discuss the "why". If the organization does not provide a reason for the changes, employees will often fill that vacuum with their own, often negative, reasons. This is true both of those impacted, and others in the organization. For example, an employee may be transferred to a new position in a new division because the new division has greater needs and the employee's skillset is a better fit. In the absence of an explanation from the company, the perception of the employee and others might be that they were not performing adequately in their existing job. This perception would lead to unnecessary pain and suffering for the employee.

Involve those impacted in the change. The person doing a job is usually the one that knows the ins and outs of that job more than anyone. They will see things in the details that can either derail the change or make it a rousing success. Further, involving them in the change can help create meaning in the new situation.

Celebrate the change. Leaders may not see the change as a big event, but chances are those impacted do. While it might seem like just another day to the leader, it is certainly more than that for those directly affected. Treating it as just another day minimizes the opportunity for employees to get closure on the old situation, and to get excited about the new. Taking time to celebrate, even if it is something as small as a lunch or cake in the break room, allows for recognition of the new situation and a solid good-bye to the old.

Communicate widely. It is important to communicate the change in situation across the broader organization, possibly including customers or vendors if the impacted employees related directly to them. The idea here is to maintain the personal networks that have formed. If all of a sudden, an employee is removed from a situation, leaving the network behind, it is hard for people to find them. This creates a vacuum in the system of connections that exist in the organization.

Side Note

Don't forget about the remote or distributed employees. Often off-site employees become "out of sight, out of mind", yet their need for compassionate and empathetic communication is arguably greater. Pay special attention to these four areas and how they relate to remote employees.

Extend presence. Being available and present is more challenging in a distributed environment for sure. The traditional approaches of open doors and walking the hallways become meaningless when employees are not physically present. Leaders need to consciously be aware of these employees, they must not succumb to "out of sight, out of mind". Leveraging technology such as the expanded use of video conferencing, IM systems, and group chats can be a great way to create the space needed for meaningful conversations.

Step up the active inquiry. This is even more important in a distributed environment. Employees are less likely to take the initiative to share when they are remote. The leader must be diligent on asking the questions and creating the opportunity for employees to communicate their thoughts and emotions.

Recognize the remote. The issues that develop in the Recognize All Levels section above exist in the remote world as well, even more so in a lot of cases. Remote employees do not have the chance to participate in the compassionate and empathetic activities that exist within the office. They will not get their cubicle decorated on their birthday, nor will there be flowers of condolence in their office after a personal loss. It is important to find creative ways to extend these activities to remote employees. See Heart-based Culture in Action for more ideas.

Communicate Big Events. Remote employees are often forgotten about during big events. The same steps show above for communicating these events apply to remote employees as well. Their lack of visibility will often leave them out of the loop, but a heart-based organization will put special focus on bringing them in.

KEY TAKEAWAYS

It is important to lay the groundwork and create an environment that enables a truly compassionate and empathetic communication system.

A heart-based organization must proactively eliminate stigmas that are often attached to the sharing of feelings and must act to prevent defensiveness or even retaliation when constructive criticism is offered.

Building compassionate and empathetic connections with others in the organization requires leaders to be present in both a physical and a psychological sense.

Two of the most powerful traits of heart-based leaders is a humble nature and the ability to listen.

Active inquiry helps leaders truly understand what an employee is going through. Active inquiry requires an openness to asking questions about what somebody is experiencing, rather than assume that their experience is the same as the leader's.

It is part of a heart-based leader's role to lead and support their employees when they need it most, whether it is work-related or personal.

A heart-based organization must consciously make efforts to extend their compassion and empathy not just to high level employees and professionals, but also to those who make the copies or perform janitorial services.

There are five steps that help communicate big events with compassion and empathy: pay attention to timing, discuss the "why", involve those impacted in the change, celebrate the change, communicate widely.

Heart-based Culture in Action

The COVID-19 pandemic, and the shutdowns that occurred as a result, had significant impact on how people dated. After reading several articles about how people were coping, it occurred to me that there were lessons for the business world as well. I read stories about how people were able to either start or continue dating relationships despite social distancing measures. It started with simple things like Zoom calls, but then some truly enterprising people took it to new levels. I read about Zoom dinner dates that not only featured two people talking over video, but also involved one of the parties ordering dinner via Postmates to be delivered to the other. I have recommended this approach to a few of my coaching clients, as a way to bring back the camaraderie that existed when everybody was in the office, and it is successful. Using this technique, leaders can now simulate the act of taking their employees out to lunch. Now, what can you do to creatively help your remote employees feel part of the team?

MAKE IT REAL

Audit your information sharing practices, are you as an organization as transparent as you could be? What else could you share?

Encourage your leadership team to be open and vulnerable with each other, once they develop this comfort level it will more easily transfer throughout the organization.

Institute a practice for the leadership team of walking around, eating meals in the break room, and other opportunities to mingle with employees of all levels.

Assess your procedures for big change events. Is a communication plan part of the procedure? Does it incorporate the five steps mentioned above?

Survey your remote employees. Are they getting the support they need? Do they feel part of the team?

CHAPTER 8:

PRINCIPLE #6 –
HAVE AN ABUNDANT MINDSET

A reality of life is that, to a large degree, our mindset determines our path. One path features scarcity and the other is filled with abundance. This is not some mystical concept where riches fall from the heavens, but as I will explain our choice in mindset has powerful implications for our culture, not to mention our lives in general. First, let me define the two mindsets.

The scarcity mindset is the belief that there will never be enough, whether its money, friendship, or other physical and emotional items. The belief is that there is a finite pie, so if somebody takes a piece there is less for everybody else. It is a fear-based belief that you will eventually run out. People with a scarcity mindset tend to cling to everything they have for fear of running out. It causes behaviors like lack of generosity or high levels of risk aversion. It leads to experiencing a life with many missed opportunities and experiences, as well as strong negative emotions.

The abundance mindset, on the other hand, focuses on the limitless opportunities available in life. The belief is that there is plenty to go around, and that somebody taking a piece does not mean there is less for everyone else. People with an abundant mindset are optimistic, generally happy, and grateful. They tend to be more creative and collaborative and as such attract people and opportunities. The abundant mindset leads to living life to the fullest, generosity, and creating memorable experiences.

An abundance mindset is important in a heart-based culture. In a heart-based culture, there is no room for selfishness or greed. Those with an abundant mindset have no need for selfishness and greed, because there is plenty of success to go around. A key ingredient in a culture of compassion and empathy is to have leaders who have an abundant mindset. The remainder of this chapter discusses what that looks like for a leader.

Make Helping Others the Main Thing

Leaders with an abundant mindset are comfortable in their own skin. They know that there is enough success to go around, so they focus on helping others. These leaders are involved in a lot of activities, with a lot of different people. They not only help their team, but they help other leaders and people throughout the organization. Because they believe that there is enough to go around, competition is not a thing. Abundant, heart-based leaders do what it takes to make people better.

Heart-based Culture in Action

I once had a chance to observe an HR leader in a large organization who has mastered the abundant mindset. She was the top-level human resources executive for the company. Her main focus was on helping people, both her own team and other leaders, become better. She took time to meet with people even at lower levels of management, sometimes even people three or four levels beneath her. She spent that time, even when it meant but she wasn't working on her own projects, because she saw her purpose in life to be helping others. These efforts led to the organization having outstanding results. Employees at all levels of the organization grew as a result of her mindset.

Create Win-Win Outcomes

At the heart of an abundant mindset is the belief that there are not automatically winners and losers. Scarcity mindset believes in a zero-sum game, there must be a winner and a loser. A heart-based leader will create win-win situations, they will look for opportunities where all involved can come out of a situation with a positive outcome. This mindset exists in both their personal and professional lives. These leaders will listen and seek to understand what a win looks like for the other party, and will take the time to work with them to ensure the solution is satisfactory for all involved.

Think Big – Make an Impact

People with abundant mindsets think big, it's part of their DNA. When someone has a scarcity mindset they become limited by fear, driving them to play it safe and think small. Epic things in business are created by thinking big and taking risk. Those with the abundant mindset get this. Leaders that understand this and adopt the abundant mindset will make a large impact on the organization.

Be Optimistic

Optimists with an abundant mindset are generally happy for other people's success because they know that there is enough to go around. They are full of encouragement and help drive positive energy through the culture. The flip side of this, however, can be dangerous for a heart-based culture. People who have a scarcity mindset tend to be competitive and resentful. If somebody else has success, then that means there is less success to go around. This causes those with a scarcity mindset to fear that there will be no success left for them, which often causes them to feel that they have to compete. This creates behaviors that obstruct others and cause pain and suffering in the workplace.

Embrace Change

Abundant mindsets also lead not only to acceptance of change, but to the embracing of change. People with this mindset appreciate that change has positive outcomes, no matter how challenging it may seem. They realize that while change may be difficult, the positive outcomes on the other side will be worth it. On the other side of the coin, those with scarcity mindsets are plagued by fear. They worry about the possible downsides of change and will take a long time to accept and buy into change. They fail to see the possibilities.

Focus on What Is Working

Most of us have seen the scarcity mindset in action. We have seen people with a victim mindset and a victim mentality. These are the people who are continually complaining, talking about how the process won't work, how so and so will never work out, and how that change will never work because change has never worked before. This mindset creates stress, anxiety, worry, resentment and many other words that you want to have nowhere near a heart-based culture. The abundant mindset, on the other hand, focuses on what works. They certainly identify things that don't work, but they do what they can to address it or minimize the problem and then they move on. They look past what doesn't work and move on to what does. At the same time, the heart-based leader will focus on gratitude. Research shows that expressing gratitude improves mental and physical well-being, and will lead to increased leadership success.

Take some time and think about your organization. How many people have abundant mindsets? How many have scarcity mindsets? The good news is that people can control their mindset. It often takes practice to change, but it can and does happen all the time. Think about what you can do as an organization to help people along this journey. Empathize with them, treat them with compassion, and help them change their mindset.

Heart-based Culture in Action

I interviewed a guest on my podcast recently who is a living example of how somebody can shift their mindset. He dealt with homelessness for 2 ½ years, living out of his car and feeling like he was drowning in misery. He also spent an additional 2 ½ years in prison. One day he decided to change his mindset. He shared with me the story of how he yelled out exactly how he was going to change his mindset to one of abundance. Since that time he has become a serial entrepreneur who has motivated and inspired thousands, and built up a substantial business.

KEY TAKEAWAYS

The scarcity mindset is the belief that there will never be enough, whether its money, friendship, or other physical and emotional items.

The abundance mindset, on the other hand, focuses on the limitless opportunities available in life.

An abundance mindset is important in a heart-based culture. In a heart-based culture, there is no room for selfishness or greed. Those with an abundant mindset have no need for selfishness and greed, because there is plenty of success to go around.

Abundant, heart-based leaders do what it takes to make people better.

People can control their mindset. It often takes practice to change, but it can and does happen all the time. Think about what you can do as an organization to help people along this journey. Empathize with them, treat them with compassion, and help them change their mindset.

MAKE IT REAL

What stories do you tell as an organization? Do they celebrate individual results and successes? Are they competition focused? Incorporate stories that celebrate leaders that make others around them better.

Do you encourage people to take risks and think big? Or do you reward those who play it safe? Rewarding people for thinking big, and not punishing them when they miss, can lead to epic developments in your organization.

Identify which of your leaders have abundant mindsets and which have scarcity mindsets. How can you help those with scarcity mindsets develop the abundant mindset?

CHAPTER 9:

PRINCIPLE #7 –
COMPASSION OVER REQUIREMENTS

Traditional management thinking has put an emphasis on making sure people are doing what they are supposed to do, making sure that they are meeting their requirements. There are many tools for this, handbooks, standard operating procedures, checklists, the list goes on. Many leaders even watch to make sure their employees are sitting at their desk at the appropriate times (I have seen some even call in from out of state to check). There is so much focus on making sure that employees follow the rules that often managers lose sight of the big picture. All of this emphasis on rules at the expense of the big picture has a detrimental effect on a heart-based culture and on the business as a whole. So, what's the alternative? Read on to find how to leverage compassion and empathy instead of requirements.

Focus on the Positive

Psychology shows that people respond differently to positive and negative stimuli. When confronted with a negative experience, the first instinct of the mind is to block it out, to shut down. This often shows up as defensiveness but will also show up as disengagement or a simmering resentment—none of these outcomes are good for the business. With this in mind, it is surprising how often leaders default to negative consequences.

What really leads to change in behavior is positive experience. Positive reinforcement is the key to improving performance. When a leader provides affirmation to an employee, it causes them to feel more optimistic and work more effectively. Neuroscience indicates that positive reinforcement

- Lowers stress and improves thinking and problem-solving
- Improves self-control
- Encourages openness to new ideas and innovation
- Increases happiness
- Improves efficiency and productivity
- Leads to trust and affinity

Long lasting change comes about as a series of moments, not as a result of a sit-down dumping of negative feedback. Knowing this, a heart-based leader who is seeking results will approach employees with a different perspective, one of compassion and empathy. They would focus continually on the positive in their employees and would constantly reinforce these positive behaviors. Over time, people remember these positive conversations (no matter how brief) and these memories inspire them to achieve more and more.

What does this look like? A few methods of positive reinforcement and affirmation:

- Individualize the approach. People are unique and will respond to different things
- Reinforce skills and competencies
- Affirm a successful personal style
- Provide context when recognizing accomplishments—tie the accomplishment to the overall mission
- Recognize in a timely manner
- Be consistent and frequent
- Affirm who they are at the core—a deep level of affirmation (things such as integrity, courage, humility)

Side Note

What happens when negative feedback occurs? Neuroscience tells us that:

- People move quickly into "fight or flight" responses
- Recipients are susceptible to negative emotions from those that are providing the feedback
- Employees become defensive and sometimes hostile
- The brain has less ability to self-reflect, accept feedback, and creatively solve problems
- Stress increases

Focus on Possibilities Over Problems

It is a part of the human experience to focus on problems. As a species we are wired to focus on dangers, which interprets to problems in the business context. This leads to the focus on adherence to rules that plagues many businesses. You must follow these rules because if you don't, we will have problems, and problems are danger, and danger is terrible. But the business reality is that problems exist, and they will continue to exist, no matter whether rules are followed or not. What is created from this problem focus is anxiety, stress, and resentment. These outcomes limit employee's ability and willingness to creatively solve the problems that exist.

A better approach is to shift the focus to new possibilities. This requires leaders to be optimistic instead of pessimistic. They will need to create hope rather than create fear, encourage rather than command. In short, they will need to be leaders and not bosses. This may be a leap for some but imagine what could be accomplished by the business if employees focused more on accomplishment rather than on checking off the box. Employees would be motivated to show their potential through creative problem solving, increasing cross-functional involvement, mentoring, and giving their best effort and performance. Leaders could focus more on providing heart-based leadership, thinking big picture, and on asking insightful questions rather than assuring compliance.

Focus on strengths

Similar to the tendency to focus on problems is the tendency to focus on weaknesses. This is common throughout the corporate world. Managers conduct performance reviews to emphasize the notorious "areas needing improvement". The presumption in this process is that the employee is flawed, and the manager will fix them. These performance reviews are another example of focusing on the negative, and they create anxiety, stress, and defensiveness (often for the leaders as much as the employees). These reviews cause employees to focus on deficits, which in turn harms employee engagement and creates cultures based on fear rather than opportunity, compassion, and empathy.

Focusing on strengths has an entirely different result. An organization that operates based on strengths can create true growth with its people and in turn its business. A heart and strength-based leader spends time with their employees to recognize their strengths rather than their weaknesses. They then work together to apply these strengths in a way that grows the individual and enhances the success of the business. The highest of performers are not usually the ones that do not have weaknesses. Instead, they are the ones that have strengths that they were able to harness and capitalize on.

In addition to being a boon for the business, focusing on strengths supports a culture of compassion and empathy. Employees that are coached into leveraging their strengths become happier, more engaged, and grow at a much higher rate.

Heart-based Culture in Action

What do Wilt Chamberlain, Shaquille O'Neal, and Bill Russell have in common? All three are in the Basketball Hall of Fame signifying their achievements a being amongst the best ever to play the sport. They also are three of the worst free throw shooters that the NBA has ever seen. A traditional management approach would be to focus on their weakness, the free throw shooting. They would get poor performance reviews, a performance improvement plan, and most likely eventually be released. Focusing on their strengths, such as outstanding low post play and rebounding, would enable them to become epic performers (which is what happened of course). Which scenario would have the best results for your business?

Compassion Over Systems

As they grow, companies often add more and more systems, policies, and procedures into their business. In many cases these are designed to ease the burden on managers, minimize legal exposure, and to create consistent treatment of employees. These are laudable ambitions for sure, but the reality is that there is a significant dark side to these systems. The logical flaw in the idea of consistent treatment is that it assumes consistent circumstances. The reality is that circumstances are often not consistent at all. People are complex, and every situation has its different nuances.

These systems can often have dire consequences for the employee. A great example of systems with a dark side are no-fault attendance point systems. The way a typical system works is that an employee is allotted a certain amount of points, after which they are terminated. An absence is typically one point, tardiness is typically half a point. The reason for the absence is immaterial, they all count the same. No matter the reason, once you get to the point limit, you are terminated.

Early in my career I was responsible for administering attendance systems. I have many examples, but one stands out to me. There was an employee, let's call her Fran for the purposes of the story. Fran was a good worker, had the company's best interests at heart, and had never missed a day. Sadly, Fran's husband was diagnosed with a critical illness and she had to miss work to take him to doctor's appointments. She was not eligible for any legal protections, so she quickly amassed eight points in the attendance system, which was the limit, and therefore the system called for her termination. This, despite the fact that she had been an exemplary employee for the majority of her time with the company.

This is the case with many systems and policy programs that cover attendance, dress code, leaves of absence, and other aspects of workplace discipline. They focus on punishment over the individual. The emphasis is on the rule being broken, not on the person behind the rule. A much better approach is to shift the focal point back to the person. Take a look at the circumstances and make decisions based on the individual situation. In Fran's case, a compassionate approach would have been to work with her as she managed her husband's illness, providing her with grace as she went through this difficult time. There is no doubt that the organization would have had a great employee at the other side of it.

Heart-based Culture in Action

I recently had the opportunity to talk with the president of a manufacturing and engineering company. The conversation at some point shifted to policies and procedures. He expressed to me that he did not believe in them (other than basic ones that are needed for regulatory reasons) and that he has removed them, for the most part, from his business. He has found that policies and procedures typically lead to a reversion to the mean. This occurs because a couple of things happen. First of all, these policies and procedures are often put in a place to manage to the relatively small amount of people who do not have the company's best interest at heart. While policies and procedures help bring these employee's performance up, they also serve to limit the achieving potential of the vast majority of employees who are engaged in the business. The policies and procedures also serve as a crutch for managers, helping them avoid the discomfort of having to handle employee problems. He prefers his organization to deal with the relatively small amount of problem employees on a one on one basis, and leave the opportunity for the rest of the employees to thrive. As a result, the company has performed very well, even in challenging times.

KEY TAKEAWAYS

There is so much focus on making sure that employees follow the rules that often managers lose sight of the big picture. All of this emphasis on rules at the expense of the big picture has a detrimental effect on a heart-based culture and on the business as a whole.

Positive experience leads to lasting change in behavior.

A better approach to achieving a heart-based culture, and business results, is to shift the focus from problems to new possibilities. This requires leaders to be optimistic instead of pessimistic. They will need to create hope rather than create fear, encourage rather than command.

An organization that operates based on strengths can create true growth with its people and in turn its business.

Policies and systems place the emphasis on the rule being broken, not on the person behind the rule. A much better approach is to shift the focal point back to the person.

MAKE IT REAL

Think about how your organization does performance management and recognition. Is it based on the negative? Is it focused on improving shortcomings? Develop a plan to begin shifting the performance management focus.

How are your leadership meetings focused? Do you emphasize correcting problems? How much time do you spend on capitalizing on opportunities? How can you make these meetings more opportunity focused?

Review your policies and procedures. Do they hold back your star performers? Are they overly rigid? Do they leave out room for context? Dive deeper, if you fully trusted your employees to do the right thing for the organization, which policies would you no longer need?

CHAPTER 10:

PRINCIPLE #8 – LEARNING FROM OTHERS

Heart-based leaders realize that they can learn from others, and that they can continue to grow and lead even more effectively. They realize that working with an open mind will lead them to become better and better. These leaders are always ready to tweak their approach, change their leadership style and welcome new strategies that might improve the business. Contrast that with many leaders who are stubborn and harden themselves against new ideas. The leaders who are growth-ready are the ones that will help drive the heart-based culture. But the need to be growth ready is not limited to leaders, it applies to everyone in the organization. The openness to learning from others is at the heart of a heart-based, growth-oriented culture.

Continually Seek Feedback

Heart-based leaders are always open to learning and they

understand and accept their limitations. They accept feedback and are self-driven to incorporate it as they work to improve their skills. This can be a tough mindset for leaders to swallow. After all, as the leader they feel that they are expected to know everything—or at least more than those around them. It takes a level of confidence and humility for a leader to be open to feedback, particularly if it comes from someone beneath them in the hierarchy or from a peer. Part of building a heart-based culture is to build an environment where leaders learn that it is ok to accept feedback from all levels.

Having the humility to seek to learn from others is a powerful aspect of heart-based leadership. A humble leader knows that they are not the smartest person in every room. And they are comfortable with that. They encourage dialog, they learn from everyone at all levels. Not only does this help the leader directly, but it also serves to build trust and respect amongst the team.

Heart-based Culture in Action

Many years ago, I had the honor of working with a great example of a leader who was willing to do what it takes to learn and grow. She had made a move from a corporate marketing position to a position where she was responsible for the sales operations and team of a large business unit. This type of move was very rare for both the company and the industry, but her openness and ability to learn from all sources was a differentiating factor for her. I was able to observe firsthand how she learned from everybody around her, from people above her, from her peers, and from the people who worked for her. Her ego never got in the way of asking questions and requesting feedback. She had enough humility to even accept unsolicited advice. As a result she was able to learn this new area quickly and achieve great success for herself and the business.

Team Growth is an Extension of Leader Growth

Heart-based leaders understand that no matter how great they may be, they are still surrounded by other skilled and smart people that can make them even better. They know that leadership requires learning, and that those around them offer a wealth of skills and knowledge. These leaders put the work in, they get out of their comfort zone, and they recognize that they can only grow their team to the extent they grow themselves.

Heart-based organizations should encourage their leaders to challenge themselves and push their boundaries. They should create an environment where leaders are comfortable asking for and accepting feedback from all levels. Leaders who leap outside of their comfort zone are the ones who will realize their potential.

KEY TAKEAWAYS

Heart-based leaders realize that they can learn from others, and that they can continue to grow and lead even more effectively.

Part of building a heart-based culture is to build an environment where leaders learn that it is ok to accept feedback from all levels.

Heart-based leaders understand that no matter how great they may be, they are still surrounded by other skilled and smart people that can make them even better. They know that leadership requires learning, and that those around them offer a wealth of skills and knowledge.

Heart-based organizations should encourage their leaders to challenge themselves and push their boundaries.

MAKE IT REAL

Evaluate how leaders in your organization learn. Do they learn from all levels? Consider building in a more formalized 360 degree learning program to further encourage this learning.

Consider how much information sharing and learning exists at the peer level. Do leaders talk frequently? Do they share knowledge and learnings? Set up a forum to encourage this, activities such as brown bag lunches or even allotted time at leadership meetings for leaders to share their expertise can create an environment that fosters peer learning.

CHAPTER 11:

MAKING IT PART OF THE CULTURE

Congratulations! You've made it through the eight principles. By now you should have a great understanding of
what it takes to have a heart-based culture, do you have
a culture of compassion and empathy. You should recognize
impact that this could have on a performance of your business, and a competitive advantage they harvest culture Will
bring. The next step is to bring these elements and principles
into your culture. This can be quite the undertaking, but the
steps below and get you moving in the right direction quickly.

Start Small

For many, making the leap to a heart-based culture will take
time. It can be a significant mindset shift with a lot of moving
parts. An important thing to remember is that the benefits
are felt long before the journey is complete. Even small moves
will begin to pay dividends, and you will find that small wins
will create momentum. The cultural shift will not follow
a linear path, it will usually begin slowly but will then see

exponential growth as it takes hold in more and more parts of the organization.

Make Compassion and Empathy Part of the Daily Routine

Start with adding compassion and empathy into the daily talk in the organization. Make it part of the language. Including it in the way the organization speaks sends a message that it matters. This is more than making announcements and proclamations, this is more about including it in the everyday conversations. Consider creating a tagline that represents what you are trying to accomplish. A simple, memorable statement will provide a compass point that the organization can rally around, as well as a conversation starter.

Incorporate the heart-based principles into daily routines. People understand how routines work, so when these routines begin to incorporate compassion and empathy the system will take over and the changes will begin to become second nature. Once routines are built around compassion and empathy it becomes much easier because it becomes part of the way the organization conducts its business. Many types of routines can incorporate heart-based principles, including communicating, decision-making, recognition and other engagement programs, hiring, onboarding, terminations, conflict resolution, and many more. Take a look at the routines in your organization, identify which lend themselves to incorporating compassion and empathy and make the changes. Over time these routines will create new organizational habits.

Side Note

Changing the routines of an organization is critical for any cultural shift. And organization can communicate a change all day long, but if it is not incorporated into the actual work of the business, the change will not last.

Create a Heart-Based Environment

Heart-based principles may meet early resistance due to perceptions that people have, especially leaders, about the nature of compassion and empathy. People might be afraid to show these traits because they do not want to be seen as weak or vulnerable. Organizations need to educate employees on the true nature of compassion and empathy. Another potential pitfall is how the organization has handled employee pain and suffering in the past. In organizations where suffering has been routinely ignored, compassion and empathy are also ignored. Organizations must pay special attention to how these situations are handled culturally.

A method that can be used to begin to change these perceptions is to manage the way in which the organization reacts to certain behaviors. Emphasize formal and informal recognition of compassionate and empathetic actions, with the goal of making these actions rewarding as opposed to costly. Make sure to celebrate compassionate and empathetic actions regularly and publicly. At the same time make behaviors that undermine the heart-based culture costly. Once people understand the implications of these behaviors, they will start to understand that compassion and empathy are desired traits and that it is possible to implement them in the workplace. Think about these actions as you make employment decisions. Promoting people that model compassion and empathy sends a strong message to the organization. Promoting people that don't model these actions also sends a strong message, albeit the wrong message.

If you don't have them already, begin to set team goals to help people understand that their success is tied to the success of their teammates. This will serve to foster a more cooperative spirit with less destructive competition.

Institute routines for how you handle failures, mistakes and near misses in your organization. The objective for these routines is to eliminate blame and emphasize learning. Failure should be seen as a learning opportunity, not an opportunity for blame.

Build in heart-based infrastructure. Develop decision frameworks to teach the organization how to make decisions in a compassionate and empathetic way. Develop metrics that provide visibility to pain and suffering in the workplace and the cost associated with it. Design organizational roles with compassion and empathy in mind. Pay special attention to roles that have a risk management element to them, make sure that they have explicit responsibility for protecting both the organization and the well-being of stakeholders including employees, customers, and vendors.

Make compassion and empathy fun. Host gatherings or meetings that engage people in the meaning of the heart-based principles as they relate to their work. Use fun as a way to ease workplace suffering by having them create new ways to respond to problems as a group in a fun and engaging manner. Use contests to create a spirit of fun competition.

Heart-Based Culture in Action

During my graduate school days, we applied to a number of jobs as part of the post grad employment process. Most of us experienced a great deal of rejection, receiving "ding letters" became commonplace. One day we threw a rejection party, where we brought in food and beverages and burned our collection of rejection letters. This served to strengthen our bonds and bring us closer as a group. Many of these connections persist today, many years later.

As the organization moves further down the path to becoming a heart-based culture, certain informal roles will emerge. Roles such as buffers, coordinators, and trackers will become part of the culture. These rules are important to make the transition more coordinated and predictable. It is important to recognize the people that are filling these roles, as it will make participation more rewarding.

Growing compassion and empathy in the organization will also encourage employees to have more contact with each other. Leaders should encourage this by organizing meet ups, lunches, and other opportunities for employees to interact with each other and to help and support each other. This will reinforce the heart-based values of the organization.

Laying this groundwork and creating an environment

that is ready for compassion and empathy is a major step in creating a heart-based culture. Once this environment is in place progress will start moving faster.

Develop Compassion Capability

Symbolic expressions of concern can be meaningful reactions to the pain and suffering of employees, whether it be personal or professional related. That being said, when the same expressions are done over and over again, they begin to lose their effect. To truly have an impact, organizations must develop the capability to respond to these situations with individualized responses. When actions taken to help ease suffering are creative and designed for the specific situation people will notice. Compassionate responses that are customized to the individual person's situation accomplish a couple of things. They help alleviate the suffering, and also they convey a sense of empathy with the suffering person. The organization cares enough to truly understand the situation and react specifically to them as opposed to sending the standard box of flowers.

Heart-Based Hiring

To sustain the progress on a heart-based culture it is important that newly hired employees fit the environment. Organizations should modify their hiring and selection routines to emphasize high-quality connections, compassion and empathy, and the heart-based principles. Incorporating these traits into hiring and selection helps the organization find talented employees that have the right cultural fit. This matters more than ever in a heart-based culture.

Side note

Most organizations have a collection of job descriptions that describe the work to be done, and the help in the recruiting and selection process. Job descriptions in a heart-based organization can be a double-edged sword. They can be a useful tool for incorporating heart-based qualifications and activities into the work and hiring routines. Be careful, however, that job descriptions do not become a vehicle for limiting the potential of your people. Job descriptions can easily become a system that limits people if it is allowed to override compassion and empathy.

Tell the Story

Business leaders, academics, and consultants will all tell you that stories are one of the most important ways that people communicate, build trust, find motivation, and share common values. Stories are a valuable tool to help people in the organization understand the direction it is headed. Find examples of compassionate and empathetic behavior and share these stories, give people real life examples of what the heart-based culture looks like. This will help them come to understand that the organization is becoming a more compassionate place and to see that their coworkers are also compassion and empathetic people. These stories will also serve to help people believe that they too can be compassionate and empathetic in the work environment.

Heart-Based Culture in Action

I once led a significant cultural shift in a large organization. There were a lot of moving parts and different constituencies involved. One of the most impactful things that we did as a company during this transition is that we brought the top one hundred leaders from around the country together for a leadership retreat. During this meeting, we had a number of leaders present their experiences and tell the stories around what they did that fit the cultural values that we were moving toward. These stories of success within the new cultural climate made a big difference with gaining acceptance and buy-in throughout the organization.

Focus on Leaders

Much of the focus of this book has been on the organization's leaders. This is because leaders play the most important role in developing a heart-based culture. An organization can spell out and communicate values of compassion and empathy, but without the leaders living it each and every day and demonstrating to employees that's those values matter these efforts are for naught. An organization that is trying to implement a heart-based culture needs to put a lot of time and effort into developing the leadership.

Leaders are also important focal points for the organization.

Employees look to them for guidance, and they often look to them for help in interpreting organization happenings. Employees also look to leaders as role models. As a result, a leader's actions are mirrored throughout the organization as a whole. A shift to a heart-based culture will not entirely be driven top down, rather it will develop from all angles of the hierarchy. However, leaders will have an outsized impact for the reasons mentioned above.

If you don't have a strong leadership team and communication between organizational levels, you may think that you are making progress, only to learn that it is falling apart underneath. Having strong leaders, who understand and buy in to the message, will help keep the culture flowing throughout the organization.

Arm your leaders with information. Understanding that employees will look to them for guidance, make sure that your leaders are prepared to deliver the message that the organization wants them to deliver. The organization should coach its leaders to model compassion and empathy at all levels. Take the time to paint a picture of how you want the heart-based culture to look like in your organization. Be very specific, make this picture relatable so that your leaders and others can understand how this applies in their particular workplace. Use this picture to guide the organization through the process. Involve your C-level executives directly with your leaders. This could be a challenge due to the busy schedules of the executives, but this involvement will produce the most engagement from your leaders and the best ideas. The executives will bring the high-level vision of the heart-based culture, while the leaders will bring ground floor knowledge of the workforce and the culture that exists today. At times these conversations may be uncomfortable but handling these uncomfortable conversations will set the tone for the culture of compassion and empathy that you are trying to create.

KEY TAKEAWAYS

The shift to a heart-based culture will yield benefits long before the journey is complete. Even small moves will begin to pay dividends, and you will find that small wins will create momentum.

Incorporate compassion and empathy into the daily talk in the organization.

Incorporate the heart-based principles into daily routines. Many types of routines can incorporate heart-based principles, including communicating, decision-making, recognition and other engagement programs, hiring, onboarding, terminations, conflict resolution, and many more.

Heart-based principles may meet early resistance due to perceptions that people have, especially leaders, about the nature of compassion and empathy.

Emphasize formal and informal recognition of compassionate and empathetic actions, with the goal of making these actions rewarding as opposed to costly. At the same time make behaviors that undermine the heart-based culture costly.

Build in heart-based infrastructure. Develop decision frameworks to teach the organization how to make decisions in a compassionate and empathetic way. Develop metrics that provide visibility to pain and suffering in the workplace and the cost associated with it. Design organizational roles with compassion and empathy in mind.

Make compassion and empathy fun.

As the organization moves further down the path to becoming a heart-based culture, certain informal roles will emerge. Roles such as buffers, coordinators, and trackers will become part of the culture.

Organizations should modify their hiring and selection routines to emphasize high-quality connections, compassion and empathy, and the heart-based principles.

Stories are a valuable tool to help people in the organization understand the direction it is headed. Find examples of compassionate and empathetic behavior and share these stories, give people real life examples of what the heart-based culture looks like.

An organization that is trying to implement a heart-based culture needs to put a lot of time and effort into developing the leadership.

Arm your leaders with information. Understanding that employees will look to them for guidance, make sure that your leaders are prepared to deliver the message that the organization wants them to deliver.

The organization should coach its leaders to model compassion and empathy at all levels.

Involve your C-level executives directly with your leaders.

MAKE IT REAL

Begin the process now. Review the key points in the book and develop a plan to make a difference TODAY. Start small, where can you have quick impact?

Share the lessons in this book with your leadership team, have an open and honest dialog about where you are today and how you can begin to introduce the heart-based culture.

Think about where your team is today. Which of your leaders incorporate heart-based principles today? Which need help?

Look at your hiring process. Do you hire heart-based leaders? How could you change your process to build this in?

What stories do you have of heart-based behavior in your organization today? How could you share these regularly?

Create a plan to develop your leaders in a heart-based way. Consider piloting it with a few to start and then expanding to the whole team.

Develop a plan to directly engage your C-suite executives in the heart-based culture. This will be a critical step to bringing it to all levels of the organization.

ONE MORE THING.....

Compassion and empathy are powerful forces. Together they can overcome indifference, insensitivity, and toxicity. A single act of compassion can change a life forever, think about the difference that an entire organization's worth of compassion and empathy can make. Compassion is the glue that binds humanity together, within an organization compassion and empathy can create bonds that are stronger than they have ever been, enabling progress that is unfathomable with the old way of doing things.

I wrote this book as a gift to you, the organization that is striving to be the best that it can be, that is looking for the edge to put it above and beyond its competition. I truly believe that the era of toxic leadership is long past, and those companies that rid themselves of this scourge and embrace the power of compassion and empathy will be the leaders of their industry. These companies will be the new benchmark, the bellwether of a new era, and will help lead society into a new world. A world where people will be encouraged to grow, to succeed, and to make the most of their potential.

The time is now. The ball is in your court. What will you make of this opportunity?

ABOUT THE AUTHOR

For over two decades Wade Thomas has served as a strategic talent executive who guides leaders to develop and shape organizations from the perspective of high-performance management coupled with compassion and empathy.

Wade's approach has helped businesses solve critical issues based on skillsets, attitudes and actions of people—the essential ingredient for building a sustainable competitive advantage. Wade's formula for success is founded on building a culture of compassion and empathy which has proven to drive business success for hundreds of organizations.

As the founder and CEO of Aim to Win, Wade has coached and consulted with hundreds of leaders who are now practicing the principles of bringing out the best in high performing individuals and teams, so that they are equipped to achieve organizational excellence and business growth.

Wade resides in Phoenix, Arizona with his family and gets invigorated by taking in a game of soccer, playing a round of golf, or hiking the local foothills.

Visit the Aim to Win website, wwww.aimtowinllc.com, to find out more about how heart-based leadership drives meaningful change in professional lives and organizations.

ADDITIONAL RESOURCES

Coaching Services

Aim to Win offers individual and group executive coaching based on Heart-Based Principles. Our coaching services help leaders incorporate these powerful behaviors into their routines, creating an environment for loyalty, engagement, and results.

Consulting Services

Aim to Win works with organizations to achieve the benefits of a culture of compassion and empathy through its proprietary Heart-Based Culture process. Whether it's a tweak to the existing culture, or a complete overhaul, we work side by side with an organization's executives to create real and lasting change.

Speaking

Wade is available to speak to your organization on the Heart-Based Principles. This program discusses what it means to have a culture led by the heart, and actions that leadership teams can take to create a culture around these values—and create sustainable competitive advantage. Participants will leave with a plan to go back and make a difference on their culture. The presentation is designed to be one hour long and can be delivered in person or virtually.

www.aimtowinllc.com

Made in the USA
Las Vegas, NV
12 May 2022

48790449R00069